Typos and All

a collection of poetry & prose

Fiona Summerville

Typos and All

First Edition

This is a work of fiction. Names, characters, places, and incidents are a product of the author's imagination. Locales and public names are sometimes used for atmospheric purposes. Any resemblance to actual people, living or dead, or to businesses, companies, events, institutions, or locales is completely coincidental.

Copyright © 2016 by Fiona Summerville

www.fionasummerville.com

Dedication

For all the gypsies...

Who turn their hearts into art,
and bare their soul scars for
all the world to see one
beautiful, heart-wrenching
word at a time.

Introduction

I came to know Fiona Summerville through her writing, and I learned much about her from her words.

I know these things:

She's kind, but never to a fault.

She's a dreamer, without ever being naïve, or sacrificing a healthy dose of knowing cynicism.

She sees hope even when all seems lost.

She's also just a little supernatural; she's a moon goddess, a shield maiden, an alseid nymph with passion to spare.

She's possessed of a thundering heart that revels both in the freedom of hopeful roaming, and the warm, welcoming solace of home.

She writes with lyrical passion and easy, elegant beauty. She pens heartache with the same deftness as she sings soaring songs of the soul. She writes poetic spells with an infectious magic. She scribes truths to light the darkest days. She'll convince you that, throughout even the trickiest of your perils, you're going to make it.

Don't take my word for it.

Read on, and know.

— Cameron Lincoln

Table of Contents

Typos and All

She's not a story to be
rewritten...

You're her lover
not an editor,
so just love her...
typos and all.

LIFE...

Morning Musings

Lover of Life

Whatever demands, joys, hardships or laughter life brings, go at and accept them with love.

Find happiness in the little blessings that pop up in the midst of life's daily challenges.

They're there, but sometimes we get too caught up in the chaos and the wishing and waiting for another time and place that we miss them.

It's fine to look forward to that vacation or the weekend, but don't hinge your happiness on them.

Live for the now...for this very moment.

For the ribbons of gold and pink streaming through your bedroom window as the day unfurls

...that first sip of that first cup of morning bliss...

Be a lover of life.

I promise...
it will love you back.

Mantra

Everyday awaken
thankful for each new breath.

Then, make a choice...

Find one thing...
just one thing to focus on,
and do beautifully.

You owe it to the Universe.
You owe it to yourself.

Good Odds

Morning's misty, golden pink
ribbons yawn and stretch across lush
fields awash with a riotous palette of
wildflower splendor.

A new day dawns, and with it hope
springs, fresh and new, conspiring with
the Universe to turn dreams into
reality.

So smile, and make ready for an
outstanding day...the odds are in your
favor.

Be Blessed

There are blessings to be found
in every moment
...every tear
...every smile
...every burst of laughter
...every encounter with another
journeying soul

It's up to you seek them out
they're waiting to be found
and yours for the taking

...find them
...take them
...and be blessed

Hope in a Cup

Morning's glory
peeks over the horizon
wake and greet her
with a hot steaming cup of hope
and a heart filled with promise

The day is yours
The possibilities are endless...

Beauty Arises

Beauty
awakens
ethereal
each morning
with haunting remnants
of dream state desires
clinging
a gentle mist around her
as she stretches
and rises
to add her gentle flame
to the day

Morning Whispers

I love the rose gold hues of morning as
they stretch and yawn across the
horizon, their whispers of gentle
encouragement filling the space between
the Dreaming and the dawn...

"Go forth and do great works, but
gently. There's no need to rush.
Linger a bit over
every moment you're given.
There will never be another like it.
Savor it before moving on."

The Precious In-Between

In the cool darkness
of those precious minutes before dawn
when the serene melancholy of the night
gently gives way
to the soft glow of optimism heralding
the coming day

It's there
in those halfway
not quite anything just yet moments
she finds herself most at home

Neither light
nor dark
neither happy
nor sad
simply there
quiet and serene
she finds her only peace
in the all too fleeting moments
of the precious in-between

Follies of the Heart

The rain pours down
in thunderous retribution
washing clean
the follies of a heart
caught musing
over never-more-to-be
moments
in the half-lit,
coffee-scented solitude
of morning

Bliss

In the soft glow of day break
as dragonflies dance
to the mockingbird's
song of joy
I stand silent,
in wonder
the warm breeze caressing
with a softly whispered
"Good morning"

And the bliss
to bear witness
to such fleeting perfection
is not lost
on a soul ever searching
for a respite
from a life
so often
overwhelming

Fleeting Beauty

The true beauty of life
is not found
in stunning landscapes
and grand vistas of the Seven Wonders
but in the tiny
all too fleeting moments
ignored by most everyday

Seek them out
Revel in them
knowing your soul
is that much richer
for baring witness
than it was
just moments before

Missed Chances

In this camera-ready
digital age
don't worry
when you miss the chance
to photograph
the joyful fox
scampering
through the glade
or the peace
of a pink-ribboned sunrise
over the misty lake

...some moments
aren't meant to be captured
they're meant
to be lived.

Terrifying Beauty

There's a terrifying beauty to be found in the uncertainty of the unknown. An honest brutality most would rather turn away from ...stagnate and fold in upon themselves rather than chance growing into an unfamiliar darkness without some inkling of what lay before them. You don't need a light at the end of the tunnel to see what's up ahead...

You are the light...

Be bold.

Shine bright.

Let the beauty of the journey unfold before you as it's meant to.

You just might find it's not so terrifying after all.

The Search

Not Lost

I'm not lost
I've simply wandered
further
into the darkness
than you care to brave.

Stars

"Maybe it's too much,"
she thought,
"to seek to soar
far and above
the fray of the everyday
mundane existence
we're handed down
at birth
and expected to perpetuate
like dutiful drones...

But, why then,
if that's the case,
do the stars call to me
by name?"

Fear of Flight

I see you there...
your white-knuckled grip
straining
against the gilded bars
of the cage
you've called home for so long.

Circling and pacing,
back and around
keening and railing
to the heavens and beyond
about breaking out
and breaking free...

Yet so caught in your martyr's play
you failed to see
the cage door was never there,
you need only to walk through.
So, then answer me this;
now that you know -

Why are you still there?

Listen

Epiphanies rarely scream.

They come to us in whispers.
Happen in the downbeats
and in the in-betweens.

They tread softly
yet with purpose
as should we.

Listen...

Grey Day Grace

In her struggle to maintain
the perception
of placid perfection she feigned,
she lost sight,
time and again,
of the wild,
infinite beauty
of the grey day grace
from which she was made.

Wildflower Soul

I went to the woods
to rediscover
the girl
with a wildflower soul
and starlight
aflame
in her eyes.

The one...

who yearns to roam,
to tarry unharried
by the trivial tick-tock
of man's repressive clocks
wherever
her vagabond spirit
may lead

and not simply dream
but implement
schemes
both pristine and profane
daring the world to take notice.
Daring...
to shake it awake.

But who somehow got
haphazardly lost
amid the chaos and rush
of the concrete
and grime
in a moment in time
we call Progress.

Layer by Layer

Layer by layer
she stripped away
the confining perception
of what should be;
tore away
at the lies of perfection
dictated
by a woefully imperfect world;
bared herself
with abandon
heedless
of the ravages of time
to reveal
the vast,
enduring beauty
of her primordial soul

Proof of Life

She thrived
on the unrequited
...the what-could-be's
but never-would's

Sought comfort
in the purgatory of longing
that turned her soul dark
as she lost herself
in the pungent acridity
of sweet maudlin revelry

Deserving of love
yet not really...
Happy enough
but only just...

The prodigal
returning
time and again
taking that faltering plunge
into the welcoming arms
of heart-rending pain

The joy of sorrow
the only proof of life
still beating
within

My Favorite Place

My soul is
a field of wildflowers
bright and chaotic,
turning,
ever searching
for the adoration
of the sun
at its brightest
most brilliant apex,
basking
naked and unashamed
beneath its rays;

with the exception of
that one lush dell
set back
amongst the trees,
foreboding
to all
but an intrepid few.

A dark place
filled
with decadent desires
not designed for the faint
but oddly enough...

the place
my soul
lingers
the most.

Just Live

Breathe...
turn,
and walk away.

Leave behind the life
steeped
in self-perpetuating chaos
and mindless chatter
and do what you were meant to do
all along

...just live

The Hope

Permanent Break

This world
is not for the faint

Day in,
day out,
the sun shines
a moment's brilliance
before slipping
again
behind clouds
laden with broken dreams
and yet
somehow...

Day in,
day out,
we persevere
through the grey days
and torrential storms
hope glimmering
in plasticine smiles
molded
in place
waiting...

Day in,
day out

...for that permanent break
in the clouds

Soul Fire

And as the fire rose in the sky
so it did in her soul
and the girl who once cowered
alone in the dark
now turned her face to the sun
and roared.

Days Like Today

On days like today
she wondered if there'd ever come a time
again
when the wonderful
outweighed
the desolate
when smiling eyes
out-shined
the shimmer of looming tears
And when the moments of quiet self-
confidence
would finally outlast
the moments of self-reproving doubt

Deep down she knew
the answer was "yes"

But on days like today
moments like those
simply seemed
just too far away

Butterfly Wings

Every heart beats in time
to the whispered hope found
in the soft sigh of butterfly wings.

Grey Days

Believe me when I say
the grey days
won't last forever

...so hold on

Just trust me
...and hold on

Hope Renewed

"Return"
the wind whispered
through the maze
of concrete and steel spires.

"Come back"
the woods called
"You've been too long gone
from your home"

And as the crow
flew she followed

Back to the place
serenity
and bare soul
converge

Where her spirit
was free
to chase fireflies
through fairy glens

And hope renewed
became rooted once more

Bleeding Bloom

A soul at peace,
still blossoms when it bleeds.

And sometimes,
the deeper the wound,
the more brilliant its bloom.

Let it Be

Sometimes it doesn't need fixing
Sometimes it's okay to just let it be
Sometimes it's just enough to dwell in
the moment

Seething or not
linger there
...reflect

Your heart's cry doesn't need to be
discounted
resolved
or let go

Eventually maybe
but for right now
...no

So cry
scream
rail against the gods if you must

Let it out
to stretch its legs and run
far and away

There's a good chance
...one day
it will stay gone

Sidewalk Blossom

A solitary flower
breaks her shell
and blooms
through the crumbled concrete
of a sidewalk crack
heedless
to being thought out of place.
Instead she makes
the place her own

Growing roots
resilient and deep
gathering strength
from the sun
on even the coldest
of gray days.
Intrepid
...faithfully awaiting
the break in the clouds.

To some
a weed,
but to others
she seems
...a tiny blossom
overflowing with love
challenging,
and quietly changing
this harsh,
decaying world.

The Kindness

Great Expectations

How can you cast curses
out upon the world
and expect blessings
in return?

Always Love

Life is a road
that can lead you astray
or lead you home
...get you lost
or get you found.
But wherever you find yourself
always step forward boldly
with a mind open,
and filled with love

Above all else
...always love.

The Real Power

There is power in kindness
...in the gentleness of hope

Real power.

In a touch
...a word
...a glance
the knowing silence
of a hug.

People won't always see it,
let alone understand it,
so they'll take it for granted
underestimate,
and berate it.

And you'll be hurt
often.
Time and again,
of that I have no doubt,
so cry if you must

But don't let the hurt turn bitter.

Don't let the hurt settle in.
If you do, it will change you
...and don't you dare let them change you
because if you do
...they win.

No Competition

Life may be a game, but it's not a contact
sport.
Nor is it a competition to best another
soul.

It's a race to be run, not against,
but alongside your fellow man.

Perhaps even slowing, when another
runner stumbles,
to offer a hand or shoulder, instead of
running on ahead.

Run the race against yourself.

Challenge yourself and no one else.

Everyone's finish line is as individual
as the race they are running.

Be kind.

And if you can't be kind, at least don't
impede...

Simply step aside.

Connected

We are all one...
all connected
by one single
invisible,
but unbreakable string

The sun,
the stars,
the red fertile earth beneath your feet,
the song bird singing,
that person you love to hate...

All of it
...bound,
entangled,
embroiled
in the conspiracy of life

We're told
we are different;
encouraged
to embrace
the uniqueness of "me"

But sometimes,
in that celebration

we lose sight of
the importance
of the greater "we"

The simple truth being...

Disrespect any one person or thing
you disrespect all
and in that moment of thoughtlessness
disrespect yourself
most of all

The Exception

It's hard sometimes,
you know,
being soft and whole
in a world overrun by the angry,
and the bitter
driven by the need to destroy
as they feed off each other's
manipulations
and shattered dreams.

But it can be done.
It must.
If hope has any chance
of regaining its foothold,
to become the norm
instead of the exception,
once again.

Threadbare Heart

A threadbare heart
still beats and bleeds,
and there are more of us out here
than you know
...so tread kindly.

Tangled Soul

Run your fingers through my soul
gently though
take care not to get too tangled

It's a tousled mass of messy knots
only some of my own making
but all mine just the same

and all
left unattended far too long

Pearls of Grace

Worn
and weary,
she carries
centuries deep
angst and joys
within an ancient
fathomless soul
allowing
only pure intention
to reemerge
pearls of grace

The Understanding

Cry Love

Let all the words
and voices fade,
save those
that cry love.

Controlled Chaos

There were times her actions and reactions were a mystery even to herself, so how could she justify the expectation and need for someone else to understand, let alone live within the controlled chaos that was her life?

Graffiti Soul

She's an underpass graffiti mural
heart pulsing
crimson chaos
as swirling riots of color
bleed into uneven concrete cracks

She suffers no fool
a switchblade
words placed
with an urban surgeon's grace
leaving them repentantly flayed

Yet cool like a summer rain
steam rising
off asphalt
her love washing clean
grime from weary hearts

Her mind thrives on commotion
sweat slicked
bodies in motion
lipstick smears and broken headboards
from kisses that go on for days

She's a masterpiece
of urbane decay
buried deep
yet still thriving
in an untamed graffiti soul

Masterpiece

She's a masterpiece
of metaphors
and unapologetic contradictions...

Comfortable in her unease
she's equal parts
sunlight and shadow
steel swathed in cashmere
guileless cunning
grounded yet always striving
to soar among the stars

...a refined and polished wild child
just trying to find her space
in a place that's not her own

Heart in Words

She writes her heart,
and sometimes
it isn't pretty.
At times
it's downright raw,
a brazen
discordant vulgarity
stripped bare
of any elegance at all.

Not written
to impress,
simply written
to express,
she writes
authentically flawed
in a world devoid of and searching
for any form
of authenticity at all.

Garden of Tears

She was always a little sad
but a beautiful sort of sad...

A type of gray
rainy day
sadness
that sometimes
poured down
around her
often muddying
the foot paths of her mind
yet that never failed
to yield
to the sun's warm rays
breaking through
melting away
the dreariness
to reveal
the lush
flourishing garden
so lovingly nurtured
by
her tears

Magic

She's at once
magic and mundane
complex in her simplicity
a bonfire
just constrained
always
threatening to break free
to set the whole damn world
ablaze

The Shadowlands

It wasn't that she was crazy or
reclusive...
she simply preferred
spending time
in the dark,
sometimes desolate,
shadowland of her mind;
to the
too loud,
too fast,
too garish
place
the world beyond
had become.

The Mirror

She fluffs her hair one last time
and glosses over her pretty pink pout
while refusing to meet the vacant eyes
that hold so many lies

Mustn't let them see me falter...
mustn't let them see me cry
They can't know I'm tired
or a crumbled mess inside

As she turns to face the world
grace and strength personified
no one ever the wiser
of her silent anguished cries

But no matter how hard she smiles
...no matter how hard she tries
the simple fact of the matter is
she's slowly dying inside

Elements

She's sky and saltwater mixed...

Crisp,
and cool
wild,
misty blue
begging to be inhaled
as you slowly drown
in her hidden depths...

Some Days

There were days
she just couldn't even
anymore

and yet
somehow
she always did

Snowbird

When people would talk about
going through hell
she'd just smile
for she knew it all too well.
She'd spent so many
of her heart's winters there,
the Devil had nicknamed her
Snowbird.

Trust Issues

It's no secret
she'd rather talk to animals
than most people

Hell,
she'd chance
the irritated retort
of the neighborhood skunk
before willingly subjecting herself
to the meaningless,
mundane pleasantries
that pass for deep thinking
amongst the local citizen collective

So, if she takes the time
...if she makes the effort
to include you in her life
please...
don't take it for granted.
It's taken a lot for her trust
...to let you in.

Don't prove her theory
of the fickle,
conditional state
of the human heart
right
...once again.

Uncommon Peace

She soon discovered
in closing her eyes
she could fade
far and away
from troubles
that plagued her waking hours

If only for a moment
behind shuttered eyes
she might find
an uncommon peace
perhaps
...almost paradise

Bring it On

It's easy to see
when she's barely hanging on
she'll stare off in the distance
...stars shooting from her eyes
as she dreams of all the places
she'd rather be than there

until gravity and reality
intervene again
dragging her back down

and she smiles and nods
a silent "bring it on"
as she buckles herself back in
for yet another go-round

Beauty & Madness

She was dreams
and logic converged
within
a saintly sinner
wildly serene
and comfortably organized
in the midst of her disarray

Beauty and madness
entwined
within a perfectly imperfect
heart
that only knew to love
no matter what

The Taskmaster

She's the type of girl who...

even when things
are at their worst
her smile isn't fake
she isn't pretending
to be alright
she truly is

...hope won't allow anything less

Gaia's Messenger

The Earth spoke through her...

Rivers gushed
with every heartbeat
breezes whispered "welcome home"
with every sigh

Glittering eyes
told of new beginnings
Every smile
brought with it hope.

Corporeal
only for this space in time,
for her spirit belonged
to the Earth

Gratitude

Another exhausting day done,
in the quiet of her room
she lay musing
smiling
in silent wonder
at the grand manipulation
perpetrated
by her mind and soul
simply so
her eyes may bear witness
to the true magic
manifest
within even the most difficult of days
and for that sheer fact alone
she drifted peacefully to sleep,
a sweet whisper of gratitude
lingering
on her softly parted lips

Melt Away

She was stronger
than anyone
...herself included
gave her credit for
standing firm long after
others would have folded

But some days
like today
she longed for someone
just a little stronger
to hold open their arms
and whisper

"Come...
let it all go.
Melt away here.
I've got you
for as long as you need."

LOVE
&
ANGST

The Joy

Until Now

We are home now...

So far from all we are
yet somehow known and so familiar
inherent to each other
soul lovers reunited...

Always
until now...

Just a memory rising
time and again
the fleeting taste
of sweet and true
so close
yet always falling short in a lover's
kiss
hints of passion
peaking
swirling
in the arms of a stranger
still always just beyond
finger tips' reach

Until now...

As words cry out
to be sought
to be lost

in the solace
only found
in the arms
of a seeker
of the same
twin flames
smoldering
white hot
burning
are all but left for dead

Until now...

Two hearts
yearning
for more
reach out
and touch
at first fleeting
yet soon engulfed
in the firestorm
of twin souls
merging
to forge
a sanctuary
of their own

Forever only in dreams
until now

Whiskey Rain

She's like nothing that you've ever seen.
Take you to heaven
on her broken wings
A strike of lightning
followed
by a soothing rain
pouring down
like whiskey burning
until she numbs your pain
She'll love you hard
and leave you wondering
where's she's been all your life
and praying
that she'll choose to stay.

The Chaser

She stared out the window
sipping her morning brew
and mused
how much sweeter it would be
with his lips
as a chaser...

Fire Dancer

She set fire to every room she entered
then simply waited
for the one daring enough
to waltz with her
through the flames

Air Stream

The only shelter she needs
is the fortress of your strong embrace

Oh...
and maybe an Air Stream on the coast

Yeah...
that'd be nice too

But only if it's filled
with the love you've made
night after night
by the bonfire light
and the waves crashing
on the shore.

Finally

Each time he saw a little further
through her sunshine and smiles facade
she let another tear fall

Not from the sadness she hid,
but from the simple gratitude of
knowing someone finally understood

The Feather

Feather soft
she landed
a mere whisper
upon his soul...

Who knew
with a single touch
something
so light and airy
could crumble
the cold facade
he'd built up
in an effort
to keep himself whole

Lead Her Home

She feels you, you know...

Even in the most desolate of places
...in the darkest recesses of her mind
when she can't see clear
to find a way out,
somehow,
from somewhere
deep within
her soul cries out
and reaches for you
and you're always there,
arms outstretched
willing and ready
to lead her home.

Just Love the Girl

Don't worry about loving her back
together...
It makes no difference
how broken she's been,
how many pieces she has hidden,
or how many shards lay scattered,
carried by the wind.

Whole or not,
she deserves all you've got
so just
...love the girl.

Not Just a Poem

She doesn't need to be
immortalized
with ink and pretty prose

She needs to be loved
with some consistency
without guile or waning ruse

...needs to know she has a place,
not some piece of paper
to call her own

And while she may indeed
cause your heart
never more to roam

Remember,

she's a woman
made of flesh and bone
not just a fucking poem

Solitude

When things
turned dark and twisted
she knew he had to go

No understanding ear
or soft shoulder
could offer consolation
the way his solitude could

And so she let him

And for that simple act alone
he loved her
all the more

The Goddess' Dance

Draped in only stardust
as the velvet night falls
she comes alive,
soul beckoning
body pulsing
waiting
for him alone

An earthbound Goddess
weaving seduction
she dances
between the standing stones
offering herself
to be taken
upon verdant rolling knoll

Her soft sighs mingle
with the sweet night breeze
as he draws near
to claim her
beneath the moon's adoring glow
kissing every wanton inch
of ivory flesh exposed

Together they writhe
unbridled slaves
desperate to sate
the dark desires they both hide
Soaring over and again
then exploding
their cries echoing through the night

Unfurling

In the soft glow of moonfall
on a shimmering sliver
she lay
quivering to life
before him
a wild flower
unfurling
indelicately coming
undone
with each lingering
lust laden kiss

lips to petal
petal to lips

Poetry to Drown In

Eyes
keen and bright
as hope
strikes
lightning
flashes across
azure skies
bleeding
into brackish indigo
turbulent and swirling
to the sound
of love's siren
luring her
far away
from familiar shores
and there
amid the roiling
ultramarine
she found
poetry
to drown in

Rest

It's ok to be tired...

...so rest
here in my arms
be still
hide away
fade away
until you're ready
for the world once more
you are safe
here in my arms

...so just rest

Whole Again

As he held her
so tightly there
she felt every jagged shard,
every frayed end
and broken piece
slowly mend,
some moving back to where they'd been
while others,
forever changed
simply found a new and better place
but all forged whole again
in the shelter of his embrace.

Quiet Champion

It's not about the fairy tale
or the errant knight
rushing in on a valiant steed.

It's about the simple man,
with the simple heart.

A quiet champion who will fight for
love. Who will stand steadfast
in word and deed.

Vanquishing and forsaking those filled
with thinly masked guile
and manipulative intent.

Making the shelter of his arms home
for the woman he loves.

Badlands

Lost
forever treading
the tightrope gently swaying
high above the valleys
of the virtuous and profane
I slipped and tumbled
deep into your primal wilderness
And there
amid the unfamiliar
sometimes treacherous carnality
of your dark and sensual badlands
found
my peace,
myself,
my home.

Worship Me

Come...
Worship me.
I will make you a believer.

Beginnings

The space between
narrows
as halted breaths,
and pounding hearts
herald
the hungry anticipation,
the trepidation,
and driving need
to surrender
sweetly
...completely
to bury memories
of old,
and cradle gently
the new ones
waiting
...aching
to be born
...a quivering universe
ready to expand
and explode to life
as two lips
collide
in that first
moment of perfection
reborn.

First Kiss

That first meeting
leading
to that first kiss
longing unfurls
in tentative exploration
revealing
desire's sweet promise of more
as lust surges
and any boundaries yet remaining
crumble silently

Soft Cotton

In the grey dawn of morning
silken skin
still warm from sleep
shivers
as desirous hands
grasp and fumble their way
once more
up and under
soft cotton
rumpled and creased
from landing
piled in a heap
eagerly discarded
just hours before

As fingers delving
Find yearning need
glistening sweetly
that glimmers to life
once more
as greedy lips replace
calloused fingertips

and soft cotton
rumpled and creased
finds itself
piled in a heap
eagerly discarded
on the floor
...once more

Fire Dance

Two gleaming souls dance
fierce and free
serpentine
fire across barren sand
they burn
setting the world alight
embers swirling
high and away
to find their place
among the stars

Solace

Sometimes all it takes
is a simple moment
to quiet the shouts of a frantic world.

You are that moment to me.

You are my solace.

You are my safe place.

Serendipity

From the stillness
serendipity
rippled
gently stirring me from stasis
and with bated anticipation
I waited,
hammer to anvil
pounding my chest,
and watched
as you,
armed only
with soulful sonnets
tattooed upon
your weary poet's heart,
emerged
from grey mist shadows
to claim
the space
left long vacant
deep inside,
and by my side,
as yours
forevermore.

Poetry

Their poetry was written
in the quiet times
the in-betweens
the lazy Sunday afternoons
stretched out on the couch
noses buried in newspapers and books
until
as if on cue
each would glance up
catch the other's eye
hold it
smile
and as their souls softly sighed
then simply returned to the place
they'd left off

Those times
the quiet
and unspoken times
were the simplest poem ever written
and yet
the most profound

Blue Sky Days

Wave after wave
may crash
heavy
upon our shore.

Engulfing us,
threatening to drag us below
the gray day waves
and undertow.

Yet
hands clasped
together,
we endure.

Eyes locked upon each other;
ever trusting in love
and the promise of
blue-sky days to come

Come Find Me

As the silver moon rose
in the clear mid-winter sky
her whispered plea
swirled high
up and away
until landing on a moonbeam
where it softly echoed
through the night...

"Come find me..."

Patient Love

He'd been there all along
in the shadowed corners
of her lonely soul

Patient
Waiting
Biding his time
Listening
for her soft footfall
just beyond the door

Breath halting
at the sound
of the lock
finally turning
Hope streaming in
illuminating her way
as she crossed the threshold to his arms

"I'm sorry it took so long,"
she whispered.
"I got lost along the way.
But it's time for you to come home now,
and help me make this heart a home.
It's time for you to stay."

Waiting

Draped
in gossamer love
unrequited
she waits for him
like summer
awaits
its debut
beneath
spring's shady bows
tinged
with rosy hues
of hope
everlasting and true

Refusing to ponder
the grey shades
of the maybe nevers
in favor
of the soft glowing
half tones
of the hopefully,
maybe
forevers...
on some summer day
...ever more.

Wasted Time

How much precious time we've wasted.
If only I'd realized sooner:
I've loved you all along.

Rain

He saw the rain in her eyes
and knew
he'd spend his remaining days
soaked to the skin
and drowning
in their beauty

Peace

He held her there,
hand pressed
to the small of her back,
her soft rhythmic breath
at the nape of his neck
breathing her peace over him.

And in that moment,
for just an instant,
he caught a glimpse
of what his life would be like
if he never let her go.

So in that moment,
in that very instant,
he decided

He never would.

Finally Home

One day you came
and for a moment
just stood
the sun's glow at your back
rendering you
an angel
on my front door step
in so many ways
an illusion

But then you smiled
and hope shined
in the upturned corner
of your crooked grin
as you held out your heart
nestled with care
in a quivering bouquet
of wildflowers
and I knew

love had finally settled
and found its way home.

Swallowed Whole

He'd always remember her as the girl
who tried to love him back to life.
The one who tried to heal his wounds
by shining her light into his darkness,
before his darkness
consumed her whole.

The Pain

Too Much of Too Much

She hated how
frequently
he
would treat her
as if
she
was the problem.

Too needy
Too clingy
Too jealous
Too greedy
Too much
or not enough
to feed the insatiable ego
he was incapable
of feeding himself

Always too much of too much of not
enough
...never enough

And being
the good little emo thing
she be
She'd cower
bow down
capitulate
and initiate

a series of apologies
not even she could believe

But she undulated
and lied
to salve
to make nice
to soothe
the fragile beast
he hid
over and again

The truth
an infrequent
unwelcome guest
in the castle of cards he'd built
that she mortared
daily
with her tears

Heavy and wet
concrete
holding her
in a place
she didn't belong
in a place
she didn't want to be

Until she lay
shattered
poured out

150

arid
and dry
ready to crumble
to be carried away
speck by emo speck
on the wind
that screamed

"It's not you
it's him!"

Because
in reality
it was
he
that was the problem

Too insecure
Too hot
Too cold
Too inconsistent
Too much
man-whore
wrapped
in a wolf skin
draped
in a sheep's
cuddly coat

Always trading up
as he worked

to bring them down
Wooing
Cooing
caging their hearts
before moving on

Yet always
outmatched
outclassed
and unworthy
of the love
bestowed upon him
and the anguish
they wasted on him
feeling
they

...were too much of too much of not
enough

Never enough
...for his narcissistic man-whore ways

Black Hole Confessional

She held the Universe in a tear drop
reaching deep
into an abyss filled with longing
as she whispered yet another
unanswered "I love you"
into the teeming
black hole confessional
on that sultry summer night

Chaser of Tears

She dismembered bad memories
with the skill of a surgeon
but none of the good intent

Cutting and dissecting
every should-have-been
and what-went wrong
into small digestible bits
she choked down
with a near empty glass
of whiskey
and a chaser of tears

Sleight of Hand

Magic like ours was never meant to last
after all it was mere illusion...
the seductive power of suggestion
followed by an adroit sleight of hand

Almost Perfect

Letting go
of almost perfect
was the hardest thing
she'd ever done

But things like him,
one so imperfectly perfect
for her perfectly imperfect world
usually are

Waiting

Draped
in gossamer love
unrequited
she waits for him
like summer
awaits
its debut
beneath
spring's shady bows
tinged
with rosy hues
of hope
everlasting and true

Refusing to ponder
the grey shades
of the maybe nevers
in favor
of the soft glowing
half tones
of the hopefully,
maybe
forevers...
on some summer day

...ever more.

Breathe

She missed the heat
of his skin against hers
and the syncopated rhythm
of their hearts
and oft-jumbled thoughts

But most of all
especially at times like these
when air seemed in short supply
she missed the whisper
of his lips across her brow
reminding her to breathe

In Mourning

Love peels away,
the heart breaks,
and once more
the mind seeks clarity
in the whys of yearning
and pining what ifs.
Ever vacillating
between
a litany
of belligerent fuck yous
and the gentle wooing
of the angst
draped heavy and black
over a soul
lost
in mourning
a dream shattered,
instead of respectfully reflecting
on the painfully peculiar way
salvation manifests,
and rescues the soul
from inevitable ruin

Regrets

The Indian Summer heat gave way
to autumn's desolation
and with it
verdant love
died
and fell
silent
aimlessly adrift
until coming to rest
on a cushion of
withered regrets
and soon smothered
by a leaden blanket of icy discontent

Find Me Again

I wish you loved me
like you did back then,
before the world crowded in
and smothered dreams
of what might been.

I wish that more than anything

...for you
...for us

to simply just be.

Please

...come find me again.

Never Enough

She only wanted to love
and be loved by him
but the Universe
and its Merchants of Chaos
had other plans

No matter
how tenacious her heart
how fervent her belief
in him
and in them
the reality came crashing down

Sometimes love really isn't enough

Hidden Hope

Hidden in her heart
a torch burns
a scorching reminder of his absence
reducing her to ash
time and again
yet still
she tends it,
fuels it,
white hot and glowing
with empty pages
of their unfinished story,
ever illuminating
the hope-littered path
that he may
someday
find his way back

Haunted

After it ended
she ran
far and away
seeking solace
from the emptiness
echoing
in the place
they'd once called their own
only to find
no matter how far she went
the torment
always waited
its whispers
the only
lonely tenants
of her haunted soul

No Difference

What hurt most was knowing
no matter how she tried,
no matter how hard she loved,
in the end

...it made no difference at all

Wine

Her heart ached
and overflowed
with too many
painful
nocturnal musings
no amount of wine
could salve

Too many should haves
she could have
let go
but stubbornly refused

...she'd take the pain they brought
over the emptiness lurking
any day

Twilight

Her scars were deep
but still she danced
in the fading sunset
of their love
refusing to ponder
the what if's any longer
focusing instead
on the tender used to be's
and sweet nothings said
before the fickle twilight fell
and his love faded
to a glowing ember
on the distant horizon

Silent Disregard

His silent disregard of her
after all their time spent
said more about him
than all the words
he'd ever whispered in the dark
when her soul was stripped bare.

Sands

The shoreline
to your ocean
ever constant
to your ebb and flow

Don't you realize?
Don't you know?
Each time you pull away
you take a tiny glittery grain of me
when you go

Little by little I'll be less
than before
my shimmery sands
too far out
too deep to recover
while you lap and caress another far off
distant shore

3 a.m.

3 am...
the witching hour
for broken, anguished souls
and their demon tormentors.

Wishes

The one remaining wish
that plagued her
after all others faded
was that he love her once more
the way he once did

However she was no fool
and knew
her unrequited dreams and hopes
were doomed to wither and die
as all the others that had come before

At least she hoped this one would

...someday soon

Dead Butterflies

Don't bother coming back again.

Whatever butterflies remain
are either stagnant
or they're dead.

Temporary Tattoo

She thought
he'd been tattooed upon her heart
but
with every tear that fell
his memory faded more each day

like chalk drawings
in the rain

King of Nothing

You there
perched high
upon your throne of half truths
draped
in a mantel of pretty, barren words
acting always the humble conqueror

Know this

You will haunt me
evermore,
but not in the pining,
poetic
unrequited love way
your needy ego
leads you to believe

More so in the bitter
unrefined
head slamming against the desk
"What the fuck was I thinking when I
fell
for his sorry ass"
brutally honest way
I doubt your fragile ego can conceive

Grace

Operate with grace;
but never naiveté.

Move on,
forgive,
but never forget the hurt
or their part in causing it

Ever.

The Fixer – Part Two

I let you go yesterday...

tore my own heart out
beat the sense
back in
washed it clean
of any lingering
misguided hope
before tucking it back
tired and worn
but beating
stronger
than ever

I'm the fixer after all,
There's no mess I can't clean up
especially one
of my own making.

Too Real

When did it all change for you?
When did it all end?

Was it as the first of many tears fell
that you realized
you only wanted her sunshine and
glitter
and not the darkness that they hide?

Or did she fall too fast
for the words you proclaimed
so the hunt became too easy
and your interest in her waned?

Or maybe, just maybe
it wasn't anything she did at all;
maybe in the end
she was just too real
and nothing like you at all.

Freedom

Suddenly
there was freedom
a sense of peace
warm and assured
descended
as the confusion and hurt
fell away

That's when I knew I could do it
that's when I knew I could walk away
not because
I didn't love you
but because
you didn't care enough
to make me stay

ERRATA...

Poems

Poems
give both substance
and flight to the spirit
emotions manically scribbled
into words on a page
manifest as
tangible wounds
deep and pooling
held open for viewing
risking ridicule
while hunting empathy
before being stitched
and set free
on the healing wings
of hope

Dear Queen...

All queens must rest

Find the man
within whose arms
your heart's kingdom
lies safe

Redemption

Redemption
for a weary soul
can only be found
in the letting go.

Tarry Here

If you please,
let me tarry here
in my solitude
for just a moment longer.

I've neither the time
nor the inclination
to walk among
the soulless pretenders,
the mere attention seekers
trying so hard
to seem real.

Prancing and dancing
baring all
but their true souls
vying for the attention
of any and all
willing to feed
their insatiable egos.

Little do they know
their vacant words
and snarling smiles
do nothing to hide
the pool of black emptiness
in which they drown.

Still,
it pains me to bear witness

So, if you please,
let me tarry here
in my solitude
for just a moment longer,
if not forever more

Work of Art

You may be broken,
torn,
frayed at every edge,
but you're still a work of art.

How can you not see that?

Cathedral

My soul's cathedral
lays hidden deep
within the silent mist

its colors
manifest
in wooded pines,
its song
carried softly
in babbling streams,
its spirit
ever-soaring
high over the backs
of cirrus clouds
and mountain peaks
with a triumphant cry.

Confessor

Every hope,
every dream,
every secret,
debauched desire,
and indelicate sin
all find their way to you.

My confidante,
My confessor,

What penance shall I tap out
upon your keys this day?

For Her

If all else failed
If all else fell away
there was one thing
she never would ignore.

That wild eyed child
whose laughter
lilted through the trees
before flying away
on tiny sparrow wings

From whose tears sprung
fields of wild flowers
to be plucked and tucked
into messy tangles of gold

Whose love of the earth
and all its creatures
feathered and furred
rivaled that of stewards of old

and whose dreams set fire
to her little world
and still lingered
deep within

For that little girl
she would forever fight
and always,
always win.

Forest Queen

I am Queen here...

My castle nestles hidden
deep within the glen
far removed
from the madness
and chaos
called progress,
created by men.

Where the sweet scent
of peat moss and pine
mingle and dance
to the lilt of the lark
and the syncopated cry
of the scrub jay
as he hops tree to tree
with no reason why.

While by night
fairies hold court
beneath
toadstools' broad eaves
by the glow of the fireflies
flitting
over lavender waves
and cool rippling streams.

This forest is my home
a place few visit
but seldom stay
and while it may seem
at times
a dark lonely place
truth be told

I'd not have it any other way.

Stories Yet to be Written

Her mind was a wonderland teeming
with stories wild and bold
wrought with intrigue and lustful
follies
all begging to be told.

And yet some days she'd simply sit
pen upon empty paper
pleading, coaxing and cajoling forth
little more than thoughtless vapor.

It vexed her to no end, and yet
she knew better than to cast blame
for her heart was a jealous jailer
and one not so easily tamed.

So, bubbling, boiling, troubling, and
toiling
she conjured her heart smitten
until it saw fit to unlock the vault
on all those stories yet to be written.

You Don't Know Her

Those who thought her aloof
simply didn't understand
how ill-suited this world truly was
for a soul like hers.

They saw judgment
where there was none,
disdain in her far-away stare.

If truth were revealed
she was only
lost in thinking,
always dreaming
of her place
and always searching
for the path
that could take her there.

Joy

Everyday
...without fail
she chose joy

Dark Winged Hope

Dark winged hope holds tight
to remnant pieces of love
still struggling to fly

Refuse to Forget

I write to remember
and sometimes
to connect
but more often than not
I write
to drown myself
deep
time and again
in feelings
I cannot
and refuse to forget

Wrapped

Come...
Wrap your soul
around mine.

Naughty by Nature

Naughty by nature
but quietly so
she urges her pen
to lead the way
down dark delicious paths
a mind molded in modesty
so often refused to go

Always pondering
the cost

Liberation
or salvation lost
to such
a delectably wicked dilemma

Lies

I watched as love burned
an effigy in tribute
to your endless lies

Sacred Flame

Let your passion burn
Honor your soul's sacred flame
let it drive and consume you

You're bound to burn too hot
and too bright for some
but not all were meant
to dance in that same light

Cherish those who bask in its glow
the kindred souls
who not only let it burn
but fuel it so it may grow

Media Matters

Yellow-tinged
sensational drivel
masquerading
as news we need to know
pablum fed
by talking heads
who dine
like well-fed swine
as ignorant
as the masses they feed
to their vital role
in disseminating
the ingredients
key
to degenerating
the land of the free
to an autocratic society
teeming with mindless rats
groveling for scraps

Misinformation
is just the beginning

Don't say you were never warned.

The Soul

The soul at rest is a magnificent thing,
its flame softly glowing
as hopes and dreams
dance and play
through the mind's hallowed halls
until ready to emerge and ignite

Burning bright
for the world to bear witness
in inevitable awe.

Broken

The broken
oft times harbor
more tenderness
than a cheerful soul.

Prison

Trapped
time and again
in a room
crammed to the rafters
with emotions and words
with no visible means of escape

No doors
no windows
just layer
after jumbled layer
stagnating
heaped
one upon the other
smothering

Yet constantly searching
for the courage
to break free

Fast Food

In this day
of fast-food fan-fic
and quiptic quotes
that pass for prose
the whip-smart mind
with a poetic heart
and soul of a sage
is a rare commodity
if not near extinct

Moon Goddess

With a quiet sigh
she rises,
languidly stretching
over verdant hills
and hushed valleys,
her diamond strewn cloak
gently dousing
the last flickering embers
of the waning day
as the Moon Goddess begins
her nocturnal reign
over poets and dreamers
who bask in the solace
of her tender glow.

Irony

Irony
is searching for truth
between the lines
of texts hidden
from prying eyes
and promises
whispered from lips
dripping
with lust-driven lies

One Fine F*ck

What makes you think
I give one fine fuck
about what you think
or have to say about me?

I stopped listening
to the voices inside
that belittled
and maligned
long ago

And your petty heart
is less consequential
than they are,
by far

so just hush

Bad-Ass Princess

Oh, she was a princess alright.

An inked up
bad ass
wild eyed
straight tequila shooting
dark princess
draped in lace and leather
who rode her men harder
than she rode her Harley,
and left them longing
for a permanent place
between her creamy
ink-stained thighs.

Every time...

Lace and sass
trump muscles and tats
every...single...time.

Speak Your Truth

Words spoken from the heart may at
times be misinterpreted, invalidated, or
even thought false, but don't let the
fear of that possibility silence you.

Speak your heart.
Speak your soul.
Speak your truth.

Even if at times your voice is little
more than a whisper echoing through a
vast, seemingly empty valley, your
message will reach the ear meant to
hear it.

Always.

Man Enough

Thanks, but no thanks.

You're free to leave.

I'm not looking
for someone
to mold me,
or fix heartaches
of the past.

As painful
as they may have been,
they made me
the beautiful mess
I am.

Now,
if you're man enough
to love that...
you may stay.

Unknown

The unknown
only remains so
to those not brave enough
to step with faith
through the obsidian veil
trusting only in their soul's flame
low and often only flickering,
to illuminate the way.

Lifeguard

Love can save
a desperate,
drowning heart

Pay to Pray

Weighted down
ever seeking
that missing
peace
we wander
tired feet stumbling
down ancient, cobbled streets
bruising our knuckles
as we pound out a prayerful tattoo
upon gnarled wood
begging acceptance
to the inner sanctum
where then we crawl
on bloodied knees
toward an alter swathed in gold
and fall prostrate before
a barker of schemes and
halcyon dreams
promising freedom from our woes
via a tithing box
burgeoning
with copper wishes
worn smooth with worry
and we buy in
paying to pray
as every whispered oath that's come

before
swirls around us
trapped
within the hallowed archways
of misguided hope
before sacrificing themselves
in the flickering flames
from a candle box

Tequila'd Sunrises

I've loved harder
than I've ever gotten back
in return.

Maybe that's why
these days
I'm running on nothing
but empty promises
and tequila'd sunrises.

Fire

While most feared the fire in his eyes
...she sought out its heat

Wolves

Run with me;
tonight
let us be wolves

Shattered Stars

Each night she shattered into stars
and littered the night sky
in hopes,
that just by chance,
he might glance up
and wish upon
the one shimmer of love
that would finally lead him home.

Rabbit Hole

The time of pinafores and crinolines
had passed,
but still the memories lingered
of winding, wooded glens and paths,
of smiling,
disappearing cats,
of harried hares,
rushing round, and marching past
the chaos of the red queen's
capricious acts

Yet undisturbed sweet Alice sat
in quiet contemplation
as the longing ache
in that forbidden place
was shaken loose
and stirred awake
in wicked dreams of the hatted man
with a hungry gaze
and fallen angel's face

So down the rabbit hole
she leapt
to escape the properly mundane
seeking madness
and the man
she'd left

bereft
in the throes
of a red velvet haze

Face to face
she landed in wonder
swaggering hip to honey pot
"You're late, my dear," the Hatter
growled
as greedy lips upon hers fell
"But no matter how long it took,
a forever's worth of seconds
is all we'll need
to make up for the time we've lost."

Firelight
(a collaborative piece with Cameron Lincoln)

Tangled desires
Shadow dance
casting
erotic murals
across walls

Heat simmers
Lust's sheen
glowing,
crackling pillars of
entwined flame

As souls
hungry to connect
tumble
with unheeded abandon
into passion's pyre

Inhibitions scorch
to ash as
bodies blaze,
a wildfire of
sizzling sensation

Twisting
flickering

together they surge,
an inferno
white-hot and wanton

Ardour rages,
settles and wanes
to satisfied
embers by
fading firelight.

Acknowledgement

It hasn't been an easy year and a half.

Cancer has a funny way of sucking the joy right out of life. And watching the man you love fight day in and day out just to maintain some sort of normalcy is a daily lesson not only in heartbreak, but also in admiration bordering on hero worship.

Through it all we've met some amazing people. Doctors, nurses, therapists, other cancer survivors and their families. All kind and inspiring in their own ways and, most importantly, instrumental in getting us where we are today. Still fighting, but getting better...

The problem is, I'm not a joiner...I'm no recluse by any stretch, but I'm one of those people who process and deal with things better alone. So, aside from the people associated with my hubby's treatment, who offered the occasional shoulder or ear to bend, I've made this journey, for the most part, alone.

I say, "for the most part" because over the past year, I found, not only an outlet in poetry, but because of the poetry I have had the great fortune to meet some of the most amazing, talented souls I now count as friends.

Fellow journeyers - poets and dreamers, all just making their way through life, and in the process making the world a better place by baring their souls in an attempt to be heard, understood, and maybe, just maybe, reach out and touch that one heart, searching, and in need.

I've also learned a lot about love, and friendship over this past year and a half.

...who to let in
...who to trust
...who to hold close
...who to allow free passage to come and go like the seasons
...and most importantly, who to show the door permanently

In *Only Dark Around the Edges*, I singled out individuals in my Acknowledgment whose help and encouragement gave me the confidence I needed to fulfill the promise I'd made to myself in 2014 - to be published, in one form or another, in 2015.

For this book, there are simply too many souls to call out individually.

So, in addition to those mentioned in *Only Dark...Lydia, Carla, Doris, J Blu, and Poet Darcy*, all whom, of course, roll over into this book, I first want to thank everyone who read the first book and encouraged me to compile a second.

I also want to thank all those precious souls who *Share the Rhetoric* every day. Your support, during a particularly ugly few weeks, when few knew me personally, but stood up for artistic expression, whatever the form, means more to me than you will ever know. I'm an elephant in that respect. I NEVER FORGET a kindness (or wrong) done. And I consider myself blessed to keep company with such amazingly talented hearts. Thank you.

There is one person I would like to thank separately, *Cameron Lincoln*.

I will forever be indebted to you, my dear friend. Without you, I may never have learned to trust my instincts about my writing. And while I still have my moments of doubt, thanks to you I've learned to write, edit, and listen. Holding back, if necessary, until the words are ready to be set free. Your heart and tolerance (lol) are only surpassed by your talent. I'm a lucky girl to have made your acquaintance.

Finally, it is my sincerest hope that those who read *Typos and All* can find a nugget or two of inspiration to carry with them through the good and bad days, especially the bad. We all have them, and sometimes it just takes another sympathetic heart to remind us, no matter how dark the moment may seem, it never lasts. There is always hope and love waiting on the other side.

Always.

- Fiona

About the Author

Fiona Summerville is a suspense writer who also dabbles in poetry.

She is a big city, Southern California girl transplanted to a small town in Texas, the location of which she affectionately refers to as "smackdab in between Podunk and Bumf---," where she lives with her husband and a menagerie of furry, perpetual two year olds.

Before deciding to chase down her dream of being a writer, Fiona made her way through the legal and corporate worlds in stilettos and pencil skirts, as both a Legal and Executive Assistant. Each career was fulfilling in its own unique way, but the call of her muses finally won out, and once she settled in Texas, she began writing in earnest.

As a lover of words, she is a great fan of all forms of writing, but never thought herself concise enough to contemplate writing poetry. It wasn't until she and her family were faced with series of serious medical crises that the Poet Muse emerged.

In her first book, *Only Dark Around the Edges* she timidly stuck her toe into the deep end of the poetry pool, touching on a myriad of topics with which we all struggle, or find ourselves in the midst of, at one time or another in life.

In her second collection, *Typos and All,* she once again addresses life's nuances but this time delves deeper, daring the reader to remember the angst, but never lose sight of the hope and love always waiting on the other side.

She is also working on collection of poetry with a decidedly naughtier theme. *The Edge of Surrender,* will be a tasty collection of some of her steamier poetry, that she plans to release just in time to heat up the holiday season.

When she's not writing, she can be found out with her horses or sipping on a glass of wine while getting lost in a spicy novel or a book of poetry penned by one of her favorite writers.

You can find her lurking on the following social media sites:

Facebook: facebook.com/FionaSummerville
Twitter: @Fiona_S_Author
Instagram: @fiosummerville

Made in the USA
Middletown, DE
18 September 2016